Colonial Times Picture Book

An Alphabetical Journey Through Colonial America for Kids

Julie Anne Savage

Copyright © 2017 by Julie Anne Savage

Green Apple Lessons Inc. Publishing

All rights reserved. No part of this book may be reproduced or transmitted in any form or by any means without written permission from the author.

Credits: Images © Adobe Stock. Resale or use of any images from this book is strictly prohibited.

ISBN-13: 978-0-692-98638-7

ISBN-10: 0-692-98638-3

Dedication:

This book is dedicated to Benjamin Nichols,
my 5th great grandfather, who fought in the Revolutionary War,
and to all future American heroes and patriots.

Introduction

Thank you for reading the *Colonial Times Picture Book - An Alphabetical Journey Through Colonial America for Kids*!

You are about to take an alphabetical journey into the life and times of early American colonists. Colonial America was a time in early American history from 1607 to 1776. The thirteen colonies were a group of British colonies on the Eastern coast of North America. England wanted to use the American colonies to grow their empire and establish new ports for trade.

Each colony had a unique history and part in the founding of our nation. Some colonies where founded by religious people wanting freedom to worship God. Other colonies were established by investors looking for more trade opportunities. As you travel through the book from letters A to Z, you will learn many fascinating aspects of everyday life for the early American settlers. Be sure to check out the back of the book for fun craft ideas and hands on projects to extend your learning. Turn the page to begin your historical journey back in time.

Anvil

Back in colonial America, almost everything was made by hand. Many craftsmen, such as blacksmiths and silversmiths, made objects out of metal. One of the tools that a blacksmith would use was called an anvil. An anvil is made out of a hard block of stone or metal, and was used to help the blacksmith forge the iron and steel. A silversmith might use an anvil to make things out of silver, like bowls, cutlery and mugs.

Apothecary

Imagine being sick and not having a hospital nearby to go to for help. That was the case in the early American colonies. There were no medical facilities to care for the sick and wounded. When a person suffered aches and pains, they would often go see an apothecary. An apothecary was similar to a modern day pharmacist and doctor.

An apothecary would use a variety of ingredients to make remedies. Many ingredients came from plants in the garden, such as lavender, feverfew and chamomile. Other ingredients were common household staples such as vinegar and honey.

Bible

The Bible was one of the most important belongings to many of the early American colonists. The Bible was used daily as a basis for worship, teaching and law making. Most children learned how to read by using passages from the Bible.

Blacksmith

A blacksmith was a tradesman who made helpful tools and items out of metal. A blacksmith would heat iron or steel to a very high temperature and forge the item into an object that could be used for everyday life. Blacksmiths often made horseshoes, nails, hammers and axe heads.

Candles

Candle making was an essential skill in the colonial days because there was no electricity. Candles were made out of tallow, which is animal fat. Long wicks were made from flax, cotton or hemp. A candle maker would repeatedly dip the wick into a wax-like mixture, then hang the candles to dry. Candles could be held alone or placed together inside a chandelier to light up an entire room. A person who made candles for a living was called a chandler.

Curd

Curd is a dairy product that is made by curdling milk. It resembles cottage cheese in form and texture. Bread, butter and cheese were common staples in a colonial home. Cows provided milk for settlers to make cheese curd and butter.

Declaration of Independence

The Declaration of Independence was a statement which announced that the thirteen American colonies were at war with Britain. A committee of five men was appointed to write down why the colonies wanted their independence and why they should be recognized as sovereign states. The writers stated that all men are created equal, and that they are endowed by God with certain rights, including life, liberty and the pursuit of happiness. On July 4th, 1776 Congress officially adopted the Declaration of Independence of America. It was signed by fifty six members of Congress.

Dutch oven

A Dutch oven is an iron cooking pot. Colonists frequently used Dutch ovens to cook food over a fire. A Dutch oven could be used for baking, boiling, making stews or roasting. In colonial times, the primary meal of the day was usually served around 12 o'clock noon. "Bubble and Squeak" was a popular meal consisting of leftover vegetables fried in a pan with mashed potatoes and leftover meat.

Embroidery

Embroidery is the craft of decorating fabric with designs stitched in strands of thread. This was a favorite past time of many early American women, who embroidered linen and cotton fabrics. Young girls would often make samplers.

Samplers were pieces of cloth that showed various examples of stitches. Samplers of this era might contain the alphabet, Bible verses and numbers.

E Pluribus Unum

The motto *E Pluribus Unum* means, "Out of many, one." This is the official motto of the United States. It refers to the fact that the United States was formed as one nation out of the thirteen original colonies. This motto was proposed by the Continental Congress in 1782, and is used on our currency and the Great Seal of the United States.

Farmhouse

The majority of people living in colonial America both lived and worked on a farm. Farming was hard work and almost everything was done by hand. Farmers grew crops such as oats, corn and tobacco. Women on the farm looked after the children, cooked, cleaned, wove clothing and made candles. Children on the farm worked by helping with the harvest and household chores.

Firecrackers

Francis Billington was a mischievous Pilgrim boy who traveled on the Mayflower. One day, while his father was away exploring the new land, Francis remained on the ship. He made some homemade firecrackers, called *squibs*, by filling the ends of duck feathers with gun powder. Francis lit the firecrackers with a slow burning fuse and set them off inside of the ship. The room in the ship where this took place was filled with open barrels of gun powder! Miraculously, Francis was unharmed.

Gourds

In early America, utensils were hard to come by, so people used gourds for making cups and bowls. A gourd is a hollowed out shell of a fruit. It comes from a type of climbing plant that is a member of the pumpkin, squash and cucumber family. Gourds are known for their very hard rinds. People would hollow out the inside of the gourds and dry them to make various utensils and instruments.

Gowns

Gowns were open fronted robes which required ladies to wear a petticoat underneath. Most of the men, women and children only had two outfits. One was worn during the week, and another was saved for Sundays and special occasions. Daily dress for boys would include a shirt, jacket and trousers (called breeches) that ran just below the knee. Girls would wear a shirt, waistcoat, petticoat and an apron.

Haystack

Haystacks, also called hayricks, were stacks of hay left in the fields to dry. Colonists used hay to feed their farm animals. They also would use hay as a stuffing inside their beds for cushioning. People would fill their mattresses each night with a sack full of hay or corn husks. The hay contained all of kinds of insects and bugs. Hence the origin of the phrase: "Sleep tight. Don't let the bedbugs bite."

Hornbook

Few American colonists could afford books to educate their children. Because there were no formal schools, children learned at home using the family Bible. A hornbook was a book made of wood or bone which contained the alphabet. Children used horn books to learn the letters of the alphabet, numbers and Bible verses.

Indians

Indians were Native Americans who inhabited the land occupied by the colonists, prior to their arrival. European settlers would negotiate with Indians for land settlements, but many times, they simply took the land by force. Indians helped the new colonists survive by sharing with them helpful farming practices. Indians were expert hunters and fisherman. They later became trade partners with the settlers, trading beaver furs, fishhooks and utensils.

Ink & Quill

Before the invention of pencils and pens, people wrote with ink and quill pens. Ink was made from indigo plants, berries and later from soot that came from burnt lamp oil.

A quill pen was made from the feather of a large bird, such as a goose. The word pen comes from the Latin word "penna" meaning feather.

Jackpudding

A jackpudding was someone who acted silly, like a clown. In Old England, jackpuddings would perform on stage and entertain people in street performances. American colonists used this word to describe people who acted foolishly.

Jamestown Colony

Founded in 1607, Jamestown was the first permanent English settlement in America. It was the capital of the Virginia Colony. It was named after King James I of England, who sent three ships to North America to settle the new colony. During the first year at Jamestown, more than half of the original settlers died due to famine and disease.

Keg

A keg is a wooden barrel that was commonly used to store and transport goods. Kegs were used to store gun powder, flour, alcohol and other necessities of life. While most early Americans were quite religious and opposed drunkenness, the colonists saw alcohol as a necessary part of life. Many used it to cure the sick, aid digestion and strengthen the weak.

Kettle

By the beginning of the 18th century, American silversmiths and blacksmiths began making kettles from silver, aluminum and copper. Colonists placed the kettles over a fire to boil water for tea or coffee. Ladies would select different herbs and fruits from their garden, to make their own teas called Liberty Teas. These were made to replace the highly taxed imported British teas.

Livestock

Livestock are animals that are raised for food and supplies. Colonists brought farm animals such as cows, pigs, goats, sheep and chickens to help them survive in the New World. These animals were kept for domestic use on the farm, but were not pets.

Loom

A loom is a machine that was used for weaving thread or yarn into cloth. The loom holds loose threads under tension, making it easier to weave them in and out. Women would make clothing out of wool for their families. Turning sheep fleece into wool is a long process. A spindle was used to twist the fibers into thread. The final process involved dying the wool and weaving it together on the loom.

Mayflower

The Mayflower was an early 17th century merchant ship that carried Pilgrims to America. The ship left England on September 6, 1620 and spent 66 days at sea. The entire voyage was marked by disease and illness. There were 102 passengers on board, including 34 children. During winter, the passengers remained on board and many suffered from an outbreak of disease. Upon winter's end, there were only 53 people still alive, out of the original 102 passengers.

Musket

A musket is a long gun fired from the shoulder. Soldiers armed with muskets were called musket men or musketeers. Men between the ages of 16 to 60 were trained to carry and use a musket. Since muskets were quite inaccurate when shooting, the musket men would make formations to maximize their firepower.

Nine Pins

Nine pin bowling was a popular game among men, women and children in the colonies. It consisted of nine wooden pins that stood in a triangle formation. The game was played on the ground or tabletop. Players would throw a wooden ball to knock down the pins. This game was brought to America by Dutch colonists.

Nosegay

Traditionally given as a gift, a nosegay is a small bouquet of flowers. Nosegays were made from a variety of flowers picked from flower gardens and used to enhance the beauty of a woman and her home. A flower bouquet was also called a *posey* and *tussie-mussie*.

Oats

Oats were a staple grain of the colonial period. Settlers arose early to complete their chores and often ate a bowl of oatmeal for breakfast. The warm porridge was called *hasty pudding* and was typically made with raisins and molasses.

Outhouse

What did early Americans do when nature called? Colonial homes did not have indoor plumbing like today. An outhouse was a small building located outside the home with a seat and hole, similar to a toilet. Outhouses often contained a shelf, which would hold a candle for lighting.

Plantations

A plantation is a large farm. Wealthy land owners in colonial America built large plantation homes with numerous rooms and living quarters. As the need for manual labor grew on the plantations, people were brought over from Britain as indentured servants. Indentured servants were forced to work on the plantation for crimes they had committed. Unfortunately, this practice later paved the way for slavery. Many Native Americans and Africans were captured and forced against their will to work as slaves on plantations.

Preserves

Keeping foods fresh was a difficult task in early America. Fruit preserves were often made from local prunes, cranberries and blueberries called *whortleberries*.

Huckleberries, grapes, strawberries and blackberries grew wild. Orchards provided plenty of fresh fruits for making sauces, pies and preserves.

Quakers

The Quakers, also known as the Society of Friends, were a religious group of people who wanted to live quiet lives that honored God as the ultimate authority. They settled in Rhode Island, Pennsylvania and North Carolina because these colonies permitted religious freedoms. The Quakers set up meeting houses where they would worship weekly. Although they were formally known as the Society of Friends, critics called them Quakers to mock how they often "quaked" or shook with religious excitement.

Quilt

Because resources were limited, early Americans made good use out of everything they owned. Clothing was rarely thrown away. Bed covers and quilts were made from old clothes that were patched together. When an item became worn or ragged, it was cut into patches and used to mend other clothing, or to make quilts and blankets.

Children might be found sleeping under a quilt sewn from fabric remnants of their grandparent's old socks or aprons.

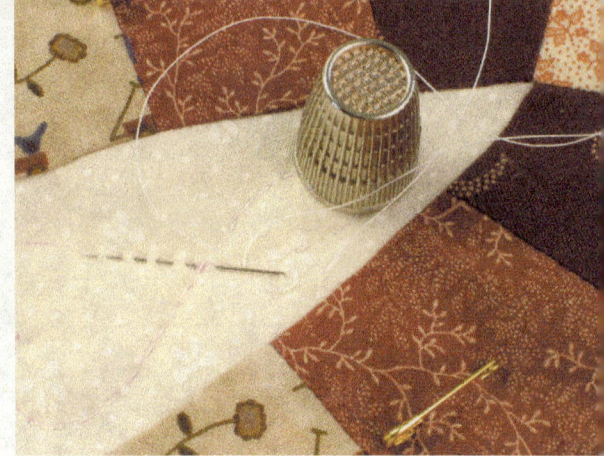

Recipes

There were no supermarkets during colonial days, so colonists had to get creative with their cooking. Popular early American recipes included Boston Baked Beans, Johnny Cakes (corn pancakes) and Hodge Podge stew. Colonial men would hunt, fish and grow crops to provide food for their families.

Reeds

Reeds are tall, slender plants that often grow near water. The coastal marshes of New England were full of reeds that colonists used to dry and make things with.

Some reeds were dried and used to make thatched roofs. Reeds were also dried and woven together to make baskets. Baskets would store household items such as utensils and yarn.

Spectacles

It wasn't until the late 1700s that spectacles came into common use in America. Spectacles are early types of eye glasses. Spectacles consisted of frames that held a pair of lenses. The earliest frames were made of wood, horn and bone. Although they were used to correct vision problems, they soon became a symbol of learning and wisdom. Benjamin Franklin needed a pair of glasses that could help him see both near and far. He invented the "double- spectacles" which consisted of a split frame holding both lenses.

Spinning Wheel

A spinning wheel is a small machine made out of wood that is used to spin yarn into thread. Many early colonists in America used spinning wheels to make their own cloth. England wanted to promote trade and discourage the Pilgrims from manufacturing their own goods. As such, England made laws forbidding the export of cloth that was made in the colonies. Laws also heavily taxed the import of spinning wheels to the colonies, which discouraged settlers from self-sufficiency.

Tobacco

Smoking tobacco was a popular pastime for many early Americans. Colonists would smoke dried tobacco leaves by using a long clay pipe, called a churchwarden. Tobacco was an important crop that helped establish the colonies in trade. Upon arriving to the New World, colonists found Native Americans growing and using tobacco, which they called *uppowoc*.

Tricorn Hat

A tricorn hat was a popular style of hat worn in colonial America. *Tri* meaning three, and *corn* meaning corners, this hat had three wide corners that were turned up along its edges. The tricorn hat was popular because it allowed colonists to show off their latest wigs. The style originated in Europe, but soon became a symbol of the American Revolution as many of George Washington's Continental Army soldiers used them as part of their uniforms.

Uniforms

A soldier's uniform would help people to quickly identify which side he was on. Colonists called the British soldiers *redcoats* and *lobsterbacks*, because of their bright red uniform coats. Early soldiers in the Continental Army did not have official uniforms, and simply wore the clothes that were on their backs. In 1775, Congress selected brown as the official uniform color for the Continental Army. Due to a shortage of brown fabric, soldiers wore blue, brown and gray uniforms.

Utensils

Wooden spoons and bowls were frequently used in cooking and were considered an important part of a home's supplies. Some utensils were made from pewter, which was more valuable so less frequently found. Common table items included iron spoons and knives. Forks were rare. The first fork brought to America was for Governor John Winthrop in Boston, Massachusetts in 1633.

Victuals

A victual is another word for food. Early colonists planted gardens and fields to maintain a steady supply of food. Common victuals included corn, pumpkins, carrots, cabbages, turnips, onions and cow cumbers, known today as cucumbers. People that lived by the sea would eat lobster, mussels, fish and clams. People who lived inland would hunt for deer, rabbits and wild game.

Violin

Violins were very popular musical instruments in the American colonies. Typically men played violins and women played harpsichords or ten string guitars. Popular violin music included ballads, folk songs, and religious psalms. American patriots who played the violin include Thomas Jefferson, Patrick Henry and Benjamin Franklin.

Wigs

Powdered wigs were popular and fashionable with men in the 18th century. Men wore wigs, called *perukes*, to appear more distinguished, and the color of the wig often identified the social class, profession or standing of the wearer. White wigs were worn by military officers and judges. Tradesmen wore brown wigs, while professionals usually donned gray wigs. Powdered wigs also helped prevent head lice which was a pervasive problem in early America.

Wooden Fifes

A wooden fife is a small, high pitched flute that is similar to a piccolo. Fifes were used in military marching bands alongside drummers. Men who played the fife were called fifers. Colonists also enjoyed using fifes to play folk music for entertainment.

X

In colonial America, Roman numerals were used on clocks and for counting. The letter X is a Roman numeral that represents the number ten. The letter V represents the number five, and the letter I represents the number one. This picture shows what colonists would see on a clock to represent the number twelve or 12 o'clock. Roman numerals were also used on coins. In 1652, Massachusetts made a set of silver coins with the Roman numerals XII. That symbolized that the coin's value was worth twelve pence or one shilling.

X-mas

X- mas is an abbreviation for the word Christmas. The celebration of Christmas in the American colonies differed from one place to another. There were many different people groups and each had their own thoughts and beliefs about the holiday. The southern colonies celebrated with parties, hunting trips and pies. The Puritans in Massachusetts, however, outlawed the celebration of Christmas because they saw it as a secular celebration not honoring to God.

Yarn

Colonial women spun yarn by hand on a drop spindle or with a spinning wheel. Many early Americans used a variety of colorful foods to dye the yarn and make clothes.

Cranberries provided red stain, and purple cabbage gave purple dye. To color the yarn, women would gather roots and berries, then boil and strain them to make the dye.

Youngsters

Children in colonial America began work and chores at a very young age. There were no formal public schools, so learning took place at the home. Older boys worked as apprentices to learn a skilled trade, such as blacksmithing. Older girls helped with domestic chores, spinning wool and child rearing. Because families were very large, children usually had many brothers and sisters to play with.

Zig Zag Fences

A zig zag fence is a type of split rail fence that was constructed out of timber logs. The logs were set at angles and rested upon one another. That created a zig zag pattern, hence the name. Zig Zag fences were used by American settlers to define property lines, divide land or contain animals in a certain area.

Zucchini

If you like to eat zucchini squash, then you would be out of luck if you lived in the American colonies. Although many colonists planted and grew many other varieties of squash such as winter squash, the zucchini squash did not come to America until Italians immigrated to the United States in the 1920s.

Colonial Crafts to Make & Do

Apothecary Cough Syrup

Materials:

1 cup of honey

1 cup of water

1/2 cup of fresh lemon juice

2 tablespoons of lemon zest

1/4 teaspoon of ground ginger (optional)

Small jar with lid

Directions:

With adult supervision, place 1 cup of water, ground ginger and lemon zest into a small saucepan. Bring the mixture to a boil. Remove from heat and allow the mixture to slightly cool. Once the temperature is still warm, but not boiling, add the honey and fresh lemon juice into the mixture. Stir the mixture to form a thickened syrup. Once the mixture has completely cooled, pour it into a sealed glass jar and refrigerate.

Use one teaspoon every 4 hours as needed for cough. Honey is not recommended for children under the age of one.

Homemade Butter

Butter is made when the fat and protein particles of cream stick together. Early American colonists used a butter churn to make butter. Even if you don't have a butter churn, you can make your own at home by following these directions.

Materials:

Heavy liquid whipping cream (room temperature)

A jar with a tight fitting lid

Directions:

Pour some of the whipping cream into a clean jar and screw on the lid. Hold the jar tightly and begin to shake the jar vigorously. Keep shaking the jar for several minutes. In about ten minutes of heavy shaking, the cream will turn into butter. Remove the butter from the jar and dispose of the remaining liquid. Store the butter in the refrigerator in a new container.

Candles

Candle making was a common practice in colonial times. While most candles were hand dipped in animal fats, you can make these beeswax candles with much less mess.

Materials:

Sheets of beeswax

Wicking

Scissors

Blow Dryer

Directions:

Lay out one sheet of beeswax and cut a wick to match the same length. If you want to make a smaller candle, just cut the wax and wick down to size.

Identify which side of the candle you want to begin rolling. Using a blow dryer, carefully heat up the side of the candle that will be rolled. As the wax begins to soften, carefully lay your wick inside the wax. Begin to roll the candle. A tightly rolled candle will be narrower than a loosely rolled one, made from the same sheet of wax. Continue to use the blow dryer to heat and roll until you reach the end of the wax. The last strip of wax should be very warm. Smooth the edges together as it cools making a tight seal.

Ink & Quill Pen

Early Americans did not have pens or pencils, but wrote instead using a quill pen and ink. If you want to experiment with what it's like to write like the colonists, try making your own ink and feather pen.

Materials:

1/2 cup of ripe blueberries

1/2 teaspoon of vinegar

1/2 teaspoon of salt

1 large feather

Scissors

Using a strainer, smash and strain the blueberries over a bowl, making sure only the juice goes into a bowl. Squeeze all of the possible juice from the berries then discard the pulp. Add the salt and vinegar to the juice. Cut off the end of a long feather at an angle, then dip the feather into the dye mixture. Use the feather to write with the ink.

Johnny Cakes

Johnny Cakes were a type of hotcakes served in colonial times. Most were served with butter and maple syrup. If you would like to try this recipe, ask your parents to help you in the kitchen. You can even make your own homemade butter using the recipe in this book.

Ingredients:

1 cup of yellow cornmeal

1/2 teaspoon of salt

1 cup of boiling water

1/2 cup of milk

Directions:

Mix the cornmeal and salt in a large bowl. Add the boiling water and stir until smooth. Add the milk and stir well. Use two tablespoons of cooking oil to grease a heavy, 12 inch fry pan. Set the pan over medium heat. Once the oil is heated, drop teaspoons of the batter into the pan and cook until golden brown. Turn the cakes and cook them on the remaining side for another five minutes. Recipe makes 12-15 small cakes.

Pomander Balls

Pomander balls are balls of fruit, studded with cloves. They were used during colonial times to decorate homes. American settlers would hang pomander balls with ribbons on a door. They also used them as festive holiday decorations. Small pomander balls were often stuffed inside a ladies handkerchief to emit a wonderful smell while traveling.

Materials:

Orange (one per person)
Toothpicks
Cloves
Decorative Ribbon
Cinnamon

Directions:

Using a toothpick, prick a hole inside the skin of an orange. Push a clove inside the hole. Repeat the process until the orange is covered in cloves. You may want to cover the entire orange, or make designs with the cloves, such as stripes or patterns. Pour a small amount of cinnamon onto a plate and carefully roll the orange in the cinnamon. The cinnamon will begin to fill the holes made by the cloves. Shake off the excess cinnamon and securely tie a ribbon around the orange. Allow the fruit to dry in a cool, dark room for two weeks until the fruit hardens.

Rose Petal Vinegar

Rose petal vinegar was a home remedy used by early Americans to treat and relieve headache pain. The formula was applied to the forehead with a rag, so that the patient could breathe in the vapors and experience some relief. Instead of applying the mixture to your forehead, pour some into your bath water for a sweet smelling and refreshing bath. Please ask an adult to help you make this craft, and be careful not to put the vinegar near your eyes.

Materials:

4 cups of white vinegar

2 cups of rose petals

1 large jar with a tight fitting lid

Directions:

Pour the vinegar into a pan. Ask and adult to bring the vinegar to a boil and then remove it from the heat. Carefully drop the rose petals into the pan allowing them to mix with the vinegar. Cool completely. Once cool, strain out the rose petals and pour the remaining liquid into a jar. Seal and store in a dark place for one week. To use with your bath, add 1/2 cup of the mixture to your bathwater.

Tin Can Lantern

Without electricity, early American colonists used candles as their main source of light. You can create your own beautiful luminaries, using tin cans and some tools from the garage. This project involves the use of hand tools so please work carefully and only with adult supervision.

Materials:

Empty soup can, cleaned with the label removed

Water

Hammer

Awl and Chisel

Tin Can

18 - 21 Gauge wire

Wire cutters

Tea light candle

Instructions:

Fill the empty soup can with water and freeze it overnight. The ice will firm up the inside of the can making it easier for punching. Place the frozen can sideways on a stable surface. You may want to place some towels underneath the can, to help absorb the shock from hammering. Use the hammer and awl to punch dotted marks on the can. Use the hammer and chisel to create lines. Don't forget to punch two holes on opposite sides of the can to attach a handle. Once completed, run the can under hot water to get rid of the ice inside. Using wire cutters, snip a portion of the gauge wire and attach it to the can as a handle. Use pliers to crimp the ends closed. Insert your tea light candle and enjoy the glow!

The Original Thirteen Colonies

1. Virginia
2. New York
3. Massachusetts
4. Maryland
5. Rhode Island
6. Connecticut
7. New Hampshire
8. Delaware
9. North Carolina
10. South Carolina
11. New Jersey
12. Pennsylvania
13. Georgia

www.ingramcontent.com/pod-product-compliance
Lightning Source LLC
Chambersburg PA
CBHW060527010526
44110CB00051B/2481